THE SHI'AR GODS SHARRA AND K'YTHRI FORCED THOR TO PARTICIPATE IN A CHALLENGE OF THE GODS. SHE WON — BUT NOT BEFORE THE GODS CALLED UPON *"THE ULTIMATE JUDGMENT,"* A POWER THEY PROMISE WILL RAZE THE UNIVERSE. KNOWING THE END MAY BE COMING, JANE MET WITH HER OLD FRIEND, ODINSON, TO FINALLY TELL HIM HER SECRET.

THERE IS MORE AT WORK THAN SHE KNOWS. MONTHS AGO, THE ULTIMATE THOR DIED DEFENDING THE MULTIVERSE. THE HERO IS GONE, BUT HIS HAMMER REMAINS. THE HAMMER OF THE WAR THOR.

AND THERE IS ONE WHO IS WORTHY.

COLLECTION EDITOR: **JENNIFER GRÜNWALD**
ASSISTANT EDITOR: **CAITLIN O'CONNELL**
ASSOCIATE MANAGING EDITOR: **KATERI WOODY**
EDITOR, SPECIAL PROJECTS: **MARK D. BEAZLEY**

VP, PRODUCTION & SPECIAL PROJECTS: **JEFF YOUNGQUIST**
SVP PRINT, SALES & MARKETING: **DAVID GABRIEL**
BOOK DESIGNER: **ADAM DEL RE**

EDITOR IN CHIEF: **C.B. CEBULSKI**
CHIEF CREATIVE OFFICER: **JOE QUESADA**
PRESIDENT: **DAN BUCKLEY**
EXECUTIVE PRODUCER: **ALAN FINE**

MIGHTY THOR VOL. 4: THE WAR THOR. Contains material originally published in magazine form as MIGHTY THOR #20-23 and GENERATIONS: THE UNWORTHY THOR & THE MIGHTY THOR #1. First printing 2017. ISBN 978-1-302-90658-0. Published by MARVEL WORLDWIDE, INC., a subsidiary of MARVEL ENTERTAINMENT, LLC. OFFICE OF PUBLICATION: 135 West 50th Street, New York, NY 10020. Copyright © 2017 MARVEL No similarity between any of the names, characters, persons, and/or institutions in this magazine with those of any living or dead person or institution is intended, and any such similarity which may exist is purely coincidental. **Printed in the U.S.A.** DAN BUCKLEY, President, Marvel Entertainment; JOE QUESADA, Chief Creative Officer; TOM BREVOORT, SVP of Publishing; DAVID BOGART, SVP of Business Affairs & Operations, Publishing & Partnership; DAVID GABRIEL, SVP of Sales & Marketing, Publishing; JEFF YOUNGQUIST, VP of Production & Special Projects; DAN CARR, Executive Director of Publishing Technology; ALEX MORALES, Director of Publishing Operations; SUSAN CRESPI, Production Manager; STAN LEE, Chairman Emeritus. For information regarding advertising in Marvel Comics or on Marvel.com, please contact Jonathan Parkhideh, VP of Digital Media & Marketing Solutions, at jparkhideh@marvel.com. For Marvel subscription inquiries, please call 888-511-5480. **Manufactured between 11/24/2017 and 12/26/2017 by LSC COMMUNICATIONS INC., KENDALLVILLE, IN, USA.**

10 9 8 7 6 5 4 3 2 1

THE MIGHTY THOR

THE WAR THOR

WRITER
JASON AARON

ISSUES #20 & #22

ARTISTS
RUSSELL DAUTERMAN & VALERIO SCHITI

COLOR ARTISTS
MATTHEW WILSON (#20, #22), **VERONICA GANDINI** (#20, #22)
& RAIN BEREDO (#22)

COVER ART
RUSSELL DAUTERMAN & MATTHEW WILSON

ISSUES #21 & #23

ARTIST
VALERIO SCHITI

COLOR ARTISTS
VERONICA GANDINI (#21) **& RAIN BEREDO** (#23)

COVER ART
RUSSELL DAUTERMAN & MATTHEW WILSON

GENERATIONS: THE UNWORTHY THOR & THE MIGHTY THOR

ARTIST
MAHMUD ASRAR

COLOR ARTIST
JORDIE BELLAIRE

COVER ART
MAHMUD ASRAR & JORDIE BELLAIRE

LETTERER
VC's JOE SABINO

ASSOCIATE EDITOR
SARAH BRUNSTAD

EDITOR
WIL MOSS

THOR CREATED ~~BY~~ : **JACK KIRBY**

OLD ASGARD.
WHERE ONCE DWELT THE GODS.

I KNOW YOU'RE HERE.

AND I KNOW YOU'RE ANGRY.

PLEASE, LET ME EXPLAIN.

WHAT IS THERE TO EXPLAIN, SENATOR FOSTER?

OR SHOULD I CALL YOU...

...THE MIGHTY THOR?

THE *OTHER* HAMMER. I HEARD ABOUT IT. I HEARD WHAT YOU WENT THROUGH TO KEEP IT SAFE FROM *THANOS* AND *THE COLLECTOR.*

AND I KNOW WHY YOU DIDN'T EVEN *TRY* TO LIFT IT.

ODINSON... I'M *AFRAID.*

IF YOU FEAR LIFTING YOUR MJOLNIR, THEN FETCH IT HERE. I'LL GLADLY TAKE IT OFF YOUR HANDS.

I'M NOT AFRAID OF LIFTING THE HAMMER. I'M AFRAID THAT THE NEXT TIME I DO...

...I'LL NEVER PUT IT DOWN AGAIN.

I HAVE *STAGE FOUR* CANCER. IT STARTED IN MY BREAST. SPREAD TO MY LYMPH NODES. MY LIVER.

I HAVEN'T BEEN FIT TO PRACTICE MEDICINE FOR MANY MONTHS. THAT JOB IN THE CONGRESS OF WORLDS I SAID I HATED...I DID IT BECAUSE IT GAVE ME A PURPOSE. IT GAVE *JANE FOSTER* A PURPOSE.

WITHOUT IT... WHAT REASON DO I HAVE TO HANG ONTO THIS...THIS RAPIDLY FAILING HUMAN FLESH?

EITHER JANE FOSTER DIES IN A HOSPITAL BED, OR I KILL HER MYSELF. BY FORGETTING SHE EVER EXISTED.

AND STAYING THE GODDESS OF THUNDER. *FOREVER.*

THAT'S WHY I'M AFRAID, ODINSON. I'M AFRAID THAT NO MATTER WHAT I DO NEXT, I'M LOSING MY--

THWHOOM

VOLSTAGG HASN'T SLEPT. HASN'T CLOSED HIS EYES. HASN'T EATEN A BITE.

HE HASN'T HEARD THE VOICE OF HIS WIFE. OR HIS FRIENDS. HIS DOCTORS. HIS CHILDREN.

HE'S SEEN THEM TALKING, THEIR LIPS MOVING, FACES FILLED WITH CONCERN.

BUT ALL HE'S HEARD IS THE ROAR OF THE FLAMES.

AND SOMETHING ELSE.

SOMETHING CALLING TO HIM.

ONLY BLOOD.

THE REALMS NEED A NEW KIND OF THOR, THE VOICE SAYS, RUMBLING LIKE DISTANT THUNDER. A THOR FOR THE TIMES.

THE WORLD TREE IS BURNING AND BLEEDING. BLOODSHED AND HORROR SPREAD LIKE WILDFIRE.

AND NO STORM CAN PUT OUT THIS BLAZE.

NO THUNDER.

21

THE WAR THOR

THE MOUNTAINS OF NIDAVELLIR ARE AS BIG AS MOONS AND AS OLD AS THE MOST ANCIENT OF STARS STILL TWINKLING IN THE HEAVENS.

TODAY THOSE MOUNTAINS ARE BURNING.

AND THE GREAT DWARF LORDS OF NIDAVELLIR, WHO ARE KNOWN FOR FORGING THE TOOLS OF WAR, ARE NOW BUSY PUTTING THEM TO USE.

SPOTTER TO MOUNT STEELSTORM! HERE COME OTHER WAVES! ALL DRAGON-GUNS OPEN FIRE!

"BLAST BUG-RIDING BASTARDS BACK TO MUSPELHEIM!"

"THERE IS TROUBLE IN THE REALMS," THE HAMMER WHISPERS.

AND JANE FOSTER ANSWERS WITHOUT A SECOND THOUGHT.

THAT IS WHY SHE IS WORTHY TO BE THOR, THE GODDESS OF THUNDER.

AND WHY SHE WILL SOON BE DEAD.

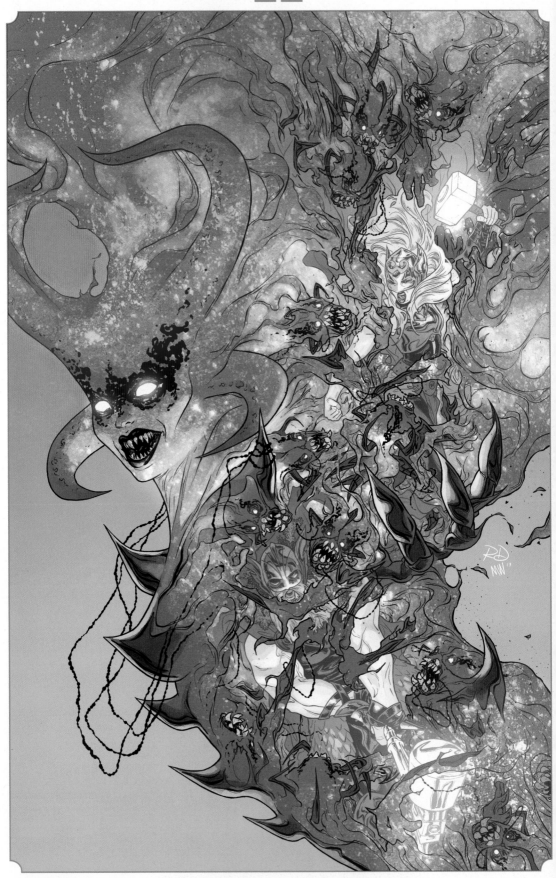

22

A FISTFUL OF BRIMSTONE

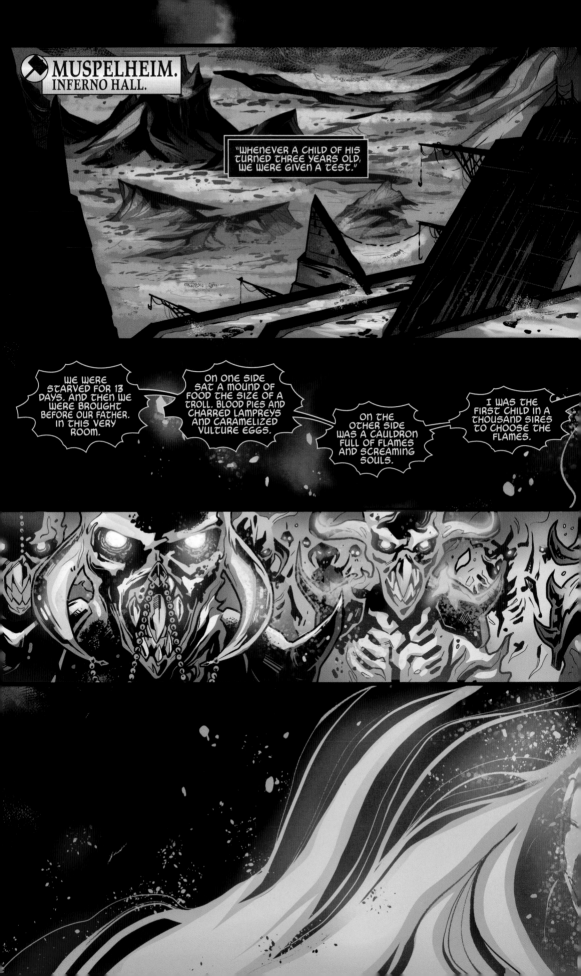

MUSPELHEIM.
INFERNO HALL.

"WHENEVER A CHILD OF HIS TURNED THREE YEARS OLD, WE WERE GIVEN A TEST."

WE WERE STARVED FOR 13 DAYS. AND THEN WE WERE BROUGHT BEFORE OUR FATHER. IN THIS VERY ROOM.

ON ONE SIDE SAT A MOUND OF FOOD THE SIZE OF A TROLL. BLOOD PIES AND CHARRED LAMPREYS AND CARAMELIZED VULTURE EGGS.

ON THE OTHER SIDE WAS A CAULDRON FULL OF FLAMES AND SCREAMING SOULS.

I WAS THE FIRST CHILD IN A THOUSAND SIRES TO CHOOSE THE FLAMES.

THE WAR OF THORS

IN THE BEGINNING, THERE WAS THE YAWNING VOID.

GINNUNGAGAP. THE GREAT UNENDING NOTHINGNESS.

AND THEN FROM THE SOUTH CAME ROARING FIRE, AND FROM THE NORTH, SWIRLING ICE AND MIST.

AND WHERE THE TWO FORCES CLASHED IN THE HEART OF THE VOID, LIFE WAS BORN.

ELVES AND GIANTS. ANGELS AND GOBLINS. GODS AND MEN.

KROOM

KRUNG

AND REALMS WERE MADE FOR EACH OF THEM. TEN IN TOTAL.

SKRRRRAAANGG

FWOOM

KRAAK

EACH WITH ITS OWN PLACE ALONG THE WORLD TREE. EACH WITH ITS OWN WONDERS AND TERRORS.

THIS IS THE STORY OF THOSE TEN REALMS.

WHUDD

GRNNGH

BAKKRAHMM

AND OF THE ONE MIGHTY GOD WHO BESTRODE THEM ALL.

KARRROOOOOAHMM

HEVEN.
THE TENTH REALM.

THERE APPEARS TO BE A STORM BREWING IN THE VOID. MOST UNUSUAL.

PERHAPS WE SHOULD RETURN TO THE PALACE, MY QUEEN.

WE ARE ANGELS IN HEVEN. WE WERE BORN TO LIVE ABOVE THE STORM.

BELIEVE ME, DEAR GIRL, SUCH TROUBLED WINDS WILL NEVER TOUCH US HERE...

"...NO MATTER HOW THEY MIGHT BLOW THROUGH THE OTHER REALMS.

SVARTALFHEIM.
THE DARK FAERIE REALM.

THE GODS ARE BOMBING THE VILLAGE! RUN INTO THE SWAMP!

SUMMON THE WAR WITCHES!

SVARTALFHEIM. THE BIRTHPLACE OF MALEKITH. THIS... IS NO ACCIDENT.

THE HAMMER BROUGHT US HERE ON PURPOSE. WHETHER YOU WILLED IT OR NOT.

MY HAMMER KNOWS THESE DARK ELVES MUST BE PUNISHED. JUST LIKE *SINDR* AND HER DEMONS IN MUSPELHEIM.

WE CAN DO THAT TOGETHER, YOU AND I. WE CAN END THIS WAR IN A *DAY*.

THIS MJOLNIR...IS SO ANGRY. SO... UNTETHERED. IT WANTS ME... TO RAGE.

THEN *RAGE*, WOMAN.

NO.

I HAVE SEEN YOUR RAGE. IN ALL ITS UGLINESS. THAT...IS NOT THE ANSWER FOR THESE TROUBLED TIMES.

WE HAVE ENOUGH WARS...

...AND ENOUGH MJOLNIRS!

BEGONE, FOUL HAMMER!

VOLSTAGG?

I'VE NO TIME FOR *JESTS,* AGENT SOLOMON.

WHAT MAKES YOU THINK I DO? AND IT'S ACTUALLY *SENATOR* SOLOMON NOW, OF THE CONGRESS OF WORLDS.

YOU'D KNOW THAT IF YOU WERE EVER... AROUND.

YOU TRULY BELIEVE VOLSTAGG IS SOME KIND OF...

I *LOOKED* FOR YOU, YOU KNOW.

WHEN YOU WERE MISSING. FOR MONTHS, I SEARCHED.

AND WHEN YOU CAME BACK, AFTER ALL THAT TIME, YOU DIDN'T EVEN... CALL OR SEND A RAVEN OR DROP BY ON YOUR... STUPID GOAT.

LADY SOLOMON, I--

ROSALIND.

YOU KNOW WHAT, *NEVER MIND.* THAT'S NEITHER HERE NOR THERE. WE'VE GOT MORE IMPORTANT THINGS TO--

OF LATE, THERE ARE MANY THINGS OF WHICH I'VE FOUND MYSELF UNWORTHY.

YOU WERE ONE.

YOU COULD'VE LET *ME* BE THE JUDGE OF THAT.

IT HURTS TOO MUCH FOR YOU TO SEE ME LIKE THIS.

WELL, I DID LIKE THE LONG HAIR BETTER. BUT ALL I REALLY SEE IS THE SAME GOD I'VE ALWAYS KNOWN.

AND, YOU KNOW...MAYBE KINDA COULDA... LOVED.

ROSALIND, I...

GENERATIONS:
THE UNWORTHY THOR & THE MIGHTY THOR

AN INSTANT APART!

A MOMENT BEYOND!

LOOSED FROM THE SHACKLES OF PAST, PRESENT, FUTURE—
A PLACE WHERE TIME HAS NO MEANING!

BUT WHERE TRUE INSIGHT CAN BE GAINED!

MAKE YOUR CHOICE! SELECT YOUR DESTINATION!

THIS JOURNEY IS A GIFT...

DR. JANE FOSTER MET ODINSON MILLENNIA AFTER HE EARNED THE HAMMER, AND THEY BECAME LOVERS, THEN FRIENDS. BUT WHEN A WHISPER COST ODINSON HIS HAMMER, JANE HEARD MJOLNIR'S CALL, FOR THERE MUST ALWAYS BE A THOR. NOW, DESPITE THE CANCER THAT IS KILLING HER MORTAL FORM, SHE DEFENDS THE REALMS AGAINST ALL ENEMIES.

THE MIGHTY THOR

THE PRINCE OF ASGARD, THE YOUNG AND HEADSTRONG ODINSON, IS DESTINED TO ONE DAY WIELD THE HAMMER MJOLNIR AS THE GOD OF THUNDER. BUT FIRST, HE MUST PROVE HIMSELF WORTHY. UNTIL THEN, HE DEFENDS THE PEOPLE OF MIDGARD, ESPECIALLY THOSE KNOWN AS VIKINGS, WITH THE AXE JARNBJORN AT HIS SIDE.

THE UNWORTHY THOR

ART BY
OLIVIER COIPEL
& JASON KEITH

THOR CREATED BY
STAN LEE, LARRY LIEBER
& JACK KIRBY

NO. THAT WAS THE *HIGHEST* I'D EVER...

YOU TRY MY PATIENCE, THOR. EVEN MORE SO THAN YOUR *WRETCHED* "BROTHER."

MJOLNIR IS NOT TO BE TOUCHED. NOT BY ANYONE. IT'S FAR TOO POWERFUL. AND TOO BOR-DAMNED *WILD!*

I JUST SAVED MIDGARD FROM AN ARMY OF RAMPAGING STORM GIANTS. I BATTLED THEM... FOR NINE DAYS STRAIGHT.

THE ONLY NOURISHMENT I HAVE TASTED...HAS BEEN MY OWN BLOOD. I THOUGHT PERHAPS I MIGHT FINALLY BE...

WORTHY.

WORTHY? YOU WISH TO BE WORTHY OF SOMETHING?

BE WORTHY OF *ME*, BOY! BE WORTHY OF BEING THE PRINCE OF ASGARD!

LOOK AT YOU, DRESSED IN *RAGS*. YOU SPEND SO MUCH TIME ON MIDGARD, YOU'RE STARTING TO *LOOK* LIKE ONE OF THOSE FILTHY BEASTS!

WE ARE RECEIVING A DELEGATION FROM VANAHEIM THIS MORN. AND YOU WILL BE THERE, LOOKING LIKE AN *ODINSON* FOR ONCE.

IN THE *THRONE ROOM*, DO YOU HEAR ME? NOT ON MIDGARD. AND NOT FOOLING ABOUT WITH HAMMERS.

NO HAMMER. NO MIDGARD. NO MEAD. THE OLD ONE-EYED BASTARD IS RUINING *ALL* MY FUN.

WHAT NEXT, NO RIDING GOATS OR HEARING...

PRAYERS.

BY YMIR'S FROZEN BEARD, WHERE ARE THESE BLASTED VANIR?

THEY'VE JUST ARRIVED, SIR. THEY'RE AT THE BIFROST NOW.

BEST SEND SOMEONE TO FETCH THEM, LEST THEY GET FRIGHTENED BY THE SIGHT OF BUILDINGS AND INDOOR PLUMBING.

THOR! GO GREET THESE BACKWOODS GODS AND BRING THEM...

THOR? WHERE THE HEL IS MY SON?!

THE PRAYER THAT SOARED ACROSS THE HEAVENS TO THE EARS OF THE THUNDER GOD...WAS A PRAYER OF DESPERATION.

A PRAYER FROM MIDGARD.

FROM ONE OF THOR'S MOST DEVOTED OF FOLLOWERS.

ONE OF THOSE FEARSOME WARRIORS OF THE NORTH KNOWN AS THE VIKINGS.

FAR HAD THEY SAILED FROM THEIR HOMES IN THE NORDIC LANDS. FARTHER THAN THEY HAD EVER SAILED BEFORE.

ALL THE WAY TO THE GREATEST RIVER IN ALL THE WORLD.

THE NILE.

THERE THEY FOUND A STRANGE LAND. UNLIKE ANYTHING THEY HAD EVER SEEN.

AND THEY DID AS VIKINGS DO.

WAAAARGH!

BUT THE LAND WAS FAR FROM UNDEFENDED.

*SEE UNCANNY AVENGERS (2012) #6!

JANE FOSTER FEELS MOST ALIVE WHEN SHE IS FIGHTING.

WHEN THERE IS SOMETHING IN FRONT OF HER SHE CAN PUNCH OR THROTTLE.

FOR SHE CANNOT THROTTLE THE CANCER THAT IS RAVAGING HER HUMAN FORM.

AND RECENTLY SHE HAS BEGUN TO WONDER...IF SHE SHOULD BOTHER HAVING A HUMAN FORM AT ALL.

WHY NOT LIVE THE LIFE OF A GOD FOREVERMORE?

WHY NOT HOLD THE HAMMER UNTIL THE END OF TIME?

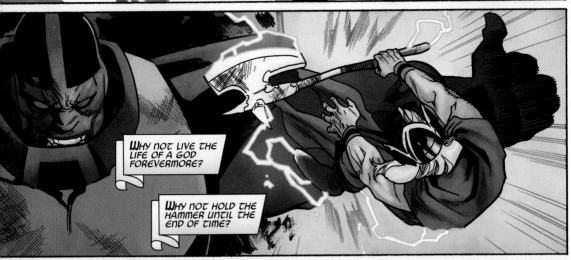

THE MORE SHE THINKS THOSE THOUGHTS, THE TIGHTER THE GODDESS OF THUNDER GRIPS HER MJOLNIR.

AND THE MORE JANE FOSTER SLIPS AWAY.

HUZZAH!

WE HAVE BESTED THE LORD OF EGYPT, AND THOR HAS STOLEN THE *NOSE* FROM THEIR RIDICULOUS LION-MAN STATUE!

ALL GLORY TO THOR, THE GOD OF THUNDER!

AYE.

ALL GLORY TO THOR.

MY FATHER DID NOT SEND YOU.

YOUR FATHER AND I...HAVE NEVER SEEN EYE TO EYE.

THEN IT WOULD SEEM WE HAVE MORE THAN A NAME AND A LOVE OF HAMMERS IN COMMON. WHO ARE YOU?

A *FRIEND*. FROM A DIFFERENT TIME.

HOW DID YOU LEARN TO CARRY THAT HAMMER?

BY WATCHING *YOU*.

ME? BAH. I CAN BARELY EVEN LIFT IT OFF THE PEDESTAL.

NEVERTHELESS, YOU PERSIST. AND I KNOW WHY.

YOU DO IT FOR *THEM*.

HMPH. THEY ARE BUT VIKINGS. I KNOW VERY MANY VIKINGS.

'TIS NOT YOUR DIVINITY THAT WILL MAKE YOU THE GOD YOU ARE DESTINED TO BECOME, YOUNG THOR.

'TIS YOUR *HUMANITY*. NEVER FORGET THAT.

YOU'RE TOTALLY GOING TO FORGET THAT.

I PLAN ON *DRINKING* UNTIL I FORGET ALL OF THIS.

THAT IS A VERY HUMAN THING TO DO.

BUT BEFORE YOU START, LET ME SAY *THANK YOU*.

THANK YOU FOR REMINDING ME...WHY I SHOULD NEVER LET GO. AND WHY I MUST--

MIGHTY THOR #20 MARY JANE VARIANT
BY **PATRICK BROWN**

MIGHTY THOR #23 ROCK–N–ROLL VARIANT
BY **MARCO RUDY**

MIGHTY THOR #23 VENOMIZED VILLAINS VARIANT
BY **CLAYTON CRAIN**

GENERATIONS: THE UNWORTHY THOR & THE MIGHTY THOR VARIANT
BY **OLIVIER COIPEL** & **JASON KEITH**

GENERATIONS: THE UNWORTHY THOR & THE MIGHTY THOR VARIANT
BY **DAS PASTORAS**

GENERATIONS: THE UNWORTHY THOR & THE MIGHTY THOR VARIANT
BY **JACK KIRBY & PAUL MOUNTS**

LA POTENTE THOR #19/#224 VARIANT COVER
BY **MAHMUD ASRAR**

fur & cape attached at armor

chain mail attached under helmet

Back

hair under

chain mail over hair & longer

- straight/thick beard, not wavy like regular Volstagg

- eyes & nose same as regular V

- eyes heavily shadowed under helmet

Height

fur & cape attached at armor

chain mail attached under helmet

Back

hair under

chain mail over hair & longer

- straight/thick beard, not wavy like regular Volstagg

- eyes & nose same as regular V

- eyes heavily shadowed under helmet

Height

- wonky anatomy,
  elongated limbs
- varied bronze
  metal pieces, spikes
  & black beaded chains
  & slightly different
  for each demon

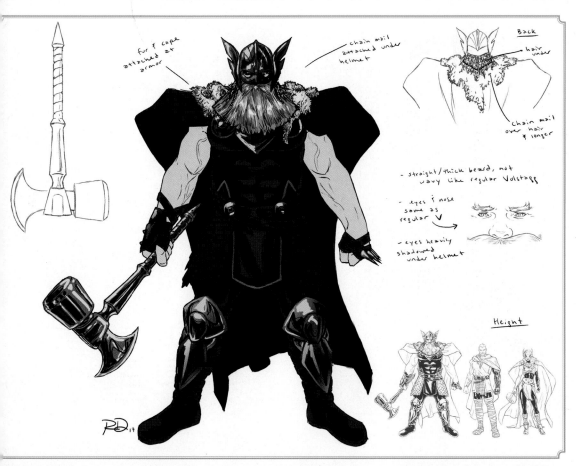

fur & cape
attached at
armor

chain mail
attached under
helmet

Back

hair
under

chain mail
over hair
& longer

- straight/thick beard, not
  wavy like regular Volstagg

- eyes & nose
  same as
  regular V

- eyes heavily
  shadowed
  under helmet

Height

#21

#22

#23

#20, PAGE 1 SKETCH

PAGE 6

PAGE 6

PAGE 8

PAGE 10

PAGE 17

THOR DESIGNS BY **MAHMUD ASRAR**

GENERATIONS COVER SKETCHES BY **MAHMUD ASRAR**